I0811913

SAINTLY RHYMES
through the year

WRITTEN AND ILLUSTRATED BY
MEGHAN BAUSCH

OSV kids
Huntington, Indiana

Copyright © 2023 by Meghan Bausch

28 27 26 25 24 23   1 2 3 4 5 6 7 8 9

All rights reserved. With the exception of short excerpts for critical reviews, no part of this work may be reproduced or transmitted in any form or by any means whatsoever without permission from the publisher. For more information, visit: www.osv.com/permissions.

Our Sunday Visitor Publishing Division
Our Sunday Visitor, Inc.
200 Noll Plaza
Huntington, IN 46750
www.osv.com
1-800-348-2440

ISBN: 978-1-68192-985-9 (Inventory No. T2720)
1. JUVENILE NONFICTION—Religious—Christian—Biography & Autobiography.
2. JUVENILE NONFICTION—Religious—Christian—Inspirational.
3. RELIGION—Christianity—Catholic.

LCCN: 2023936372

Cover and interior design: Lindsey Riesen
Cover and interior art: Meghan Bausch

PRINTED IN TURKEY

DEDICATED TO OUR BLESSED MOTHER
AND TO THE THREE CHILDREN THAT
HAVE MADE ME A MOTHER

January 21

St. Agnes

The virtuous St. Agnes,
whom many men admired,
made it known that Christ alone
was all that she desired.

Before the pure, sweet maiden
was martyred by the sword,
this innocent lamb declared, "I am
already the spouse of the Lord."

January 28

St. Thomas Aquinas

St. Thomas was a friar
who had a brilliant mind.
He studied, taught, and wrote a lot
of God and all mankind.

He proved to countless people
God really does exist
and gave us lovely Latin hymns
about the Eucharist.

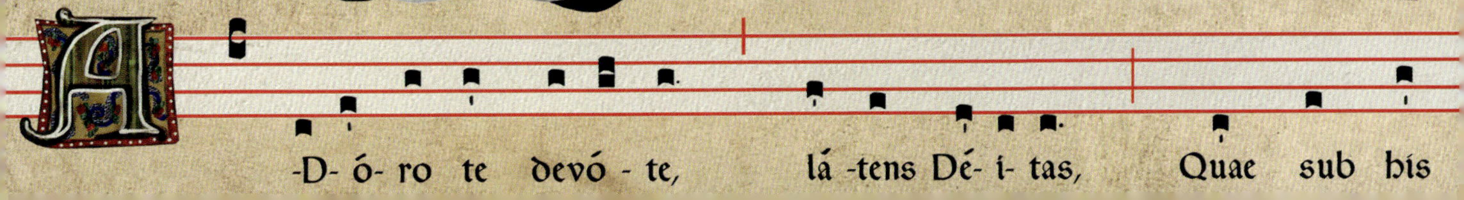

February 1

St. Brigid of Ireland

St. Brigid is the patron
of Ireland and dairy.
To spread the Faith, she founded a
great Irish monastery.

She gathered milk and butter
and gave it to the poor,
but despite her generosity
was always blessed with more.

February 6

St. Paul Miki and Companions

Paul Miki was a Christian,
an eloquent, Japanese man,
but being a Christian was frowned upon
by the Emperor of Japan.

Paul secretly studied Scripture
with several Jesuit brothers.
He courageously died when crucified
along with twenty-five others.

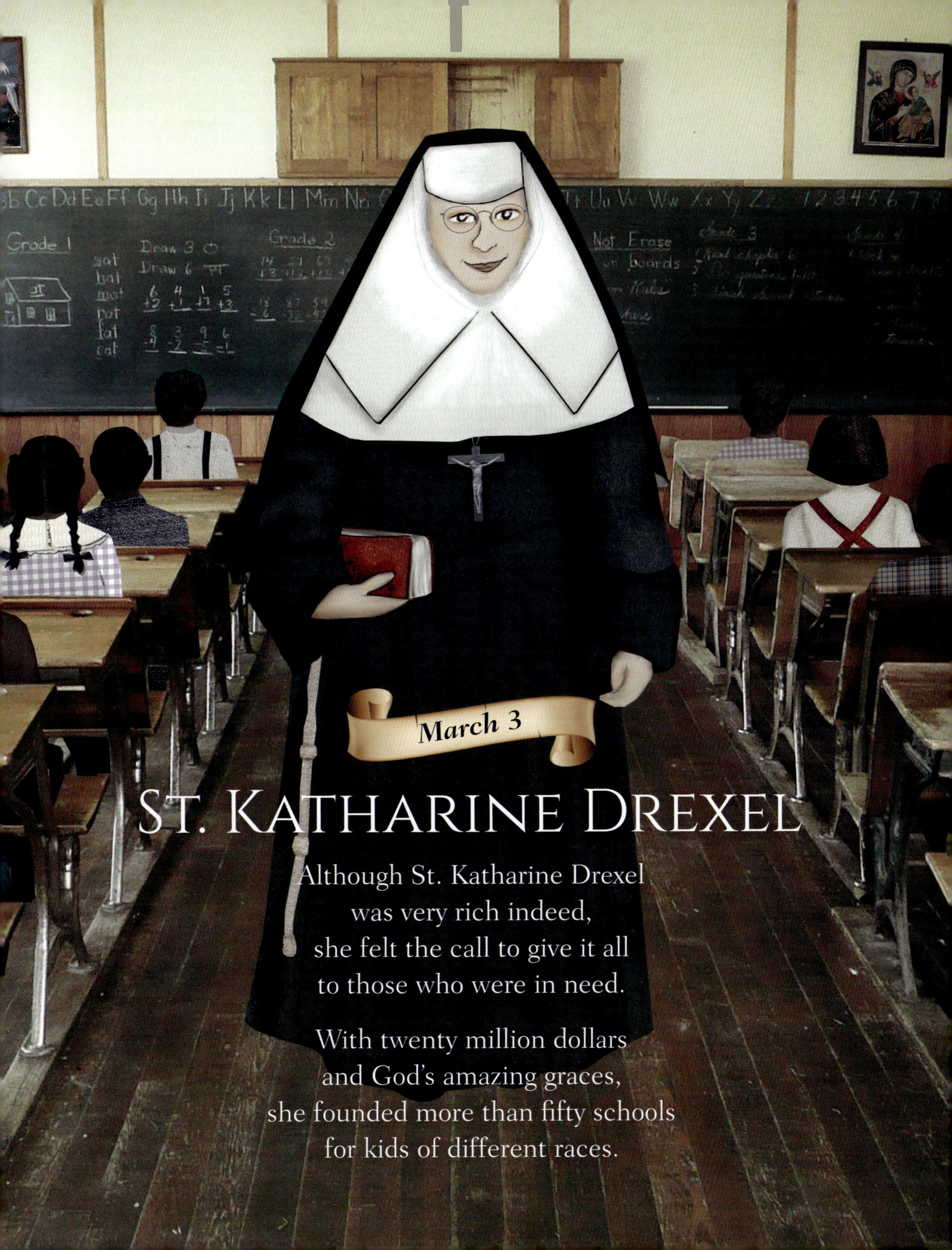

March 3

St. Katharine Drexel

Although St. Katharine Drexel
was very rich indeed,
she felt the call to give it all
to those who were in need.

With twenty million dollars
and God's amazing graces,
she founded more than fifty schools
for kids of different races.

March 19

St. Joseph

The chaste and humble Joseph
was skilled in carpentry
and chosen as protector of
the Holy Family.

The greatest foster-father
Our Savior could have had,
St. Joseph prays for those who work
as well as every dad.

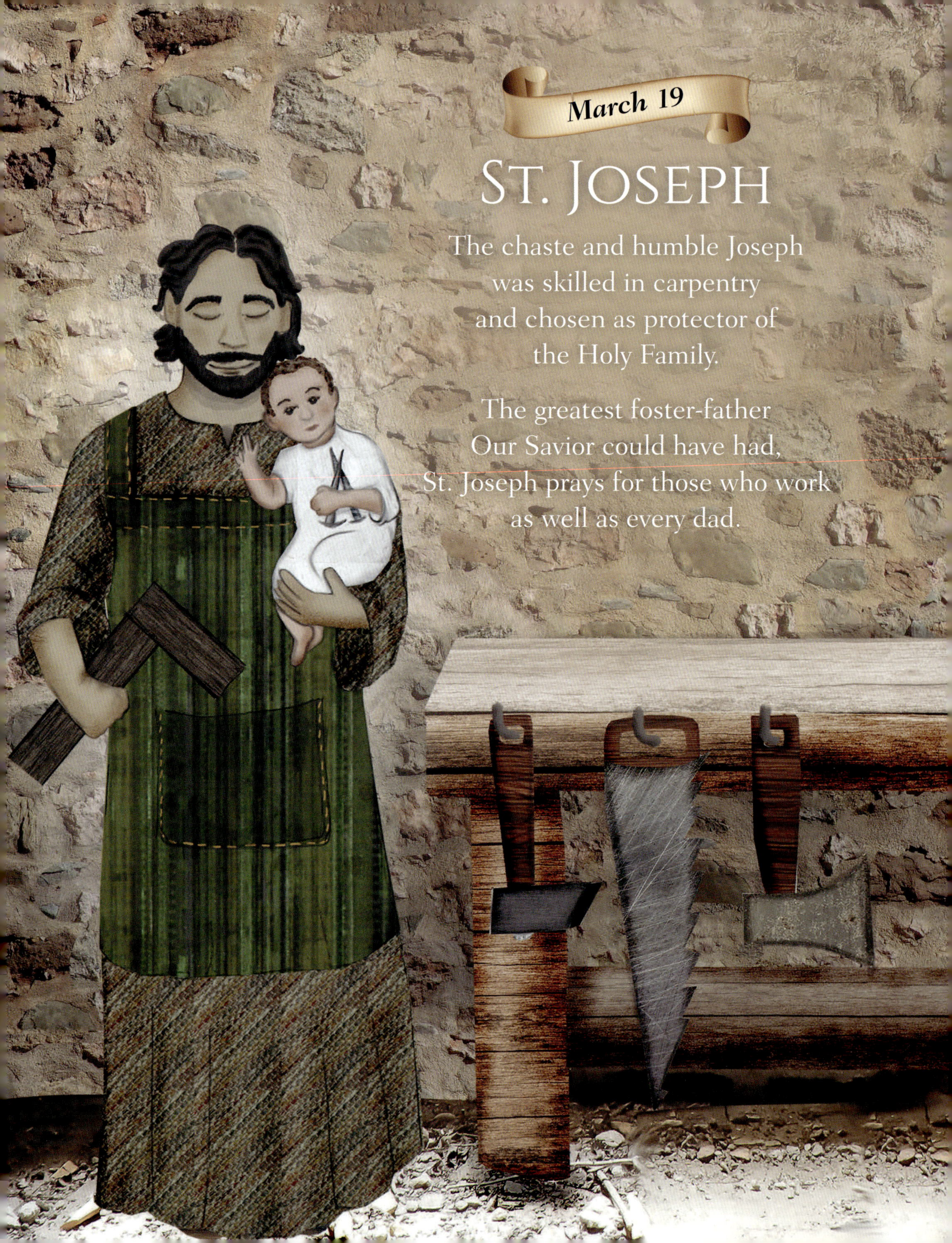

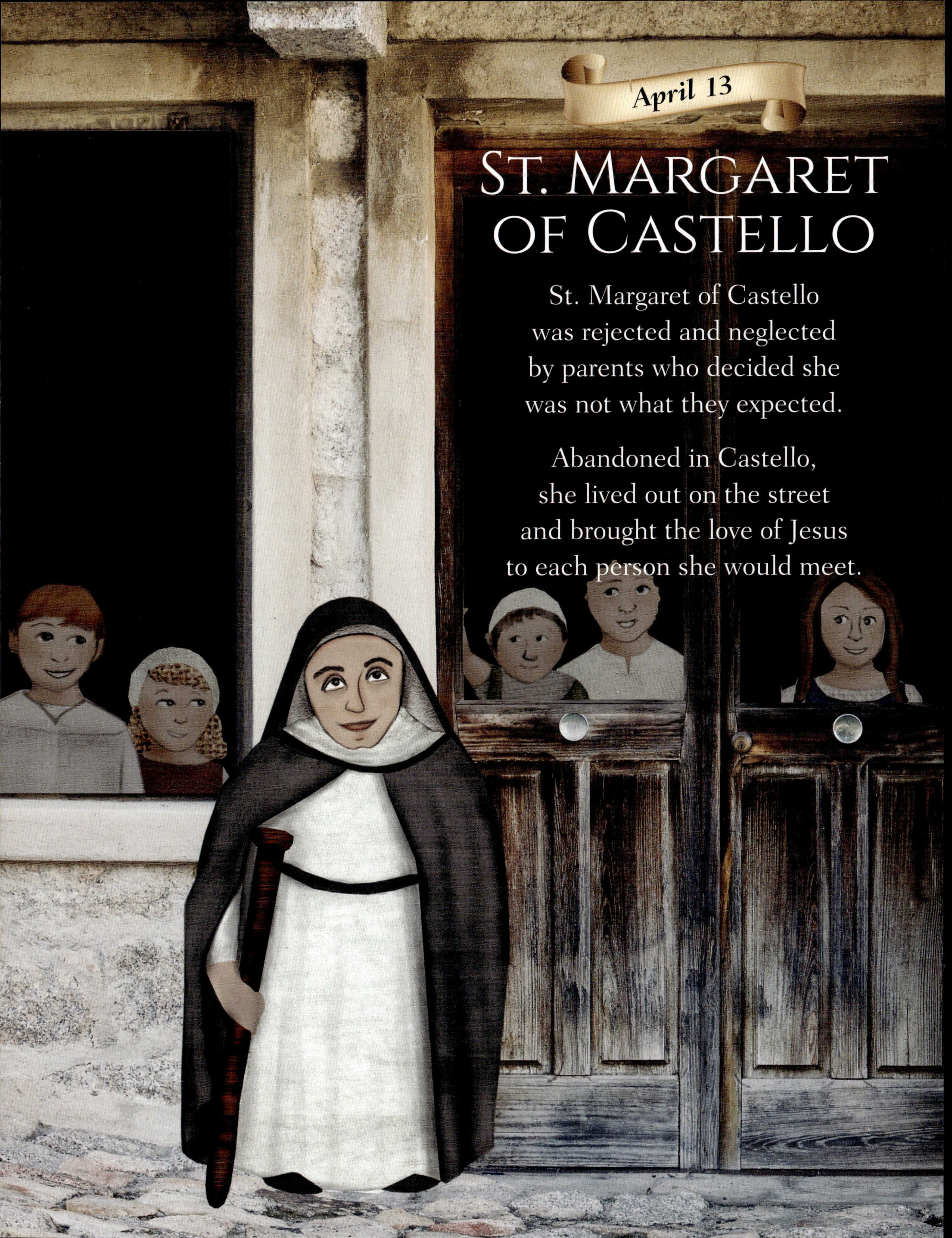

April 13

St. Margaret of Castello

St. Margaret of Castello
was rejected and neglected
by parents who decided she
was not what they expected.

Abandoned in Castello,
she lived out on the street
and brought the love of Jesus
to each person she would meet.

April 23

St. George

St. George, the mighty soldier,
and faithful Christian, too,
was martyred for defending God
and all the Church holds true.

Though George is often pictured
as a dragon-slaying knight,
the dragon's meant to represent
the evils we must fight.

May 26

ST. PHILIP NERI

The patron saint of humor,
Philip Neri lived in Rome.
His heart expanded while he prayed
down in the catacomb.

His laughs and pranks were cheerful
and all for God's great glory.
He formed a congregation that
we call the Oratory.

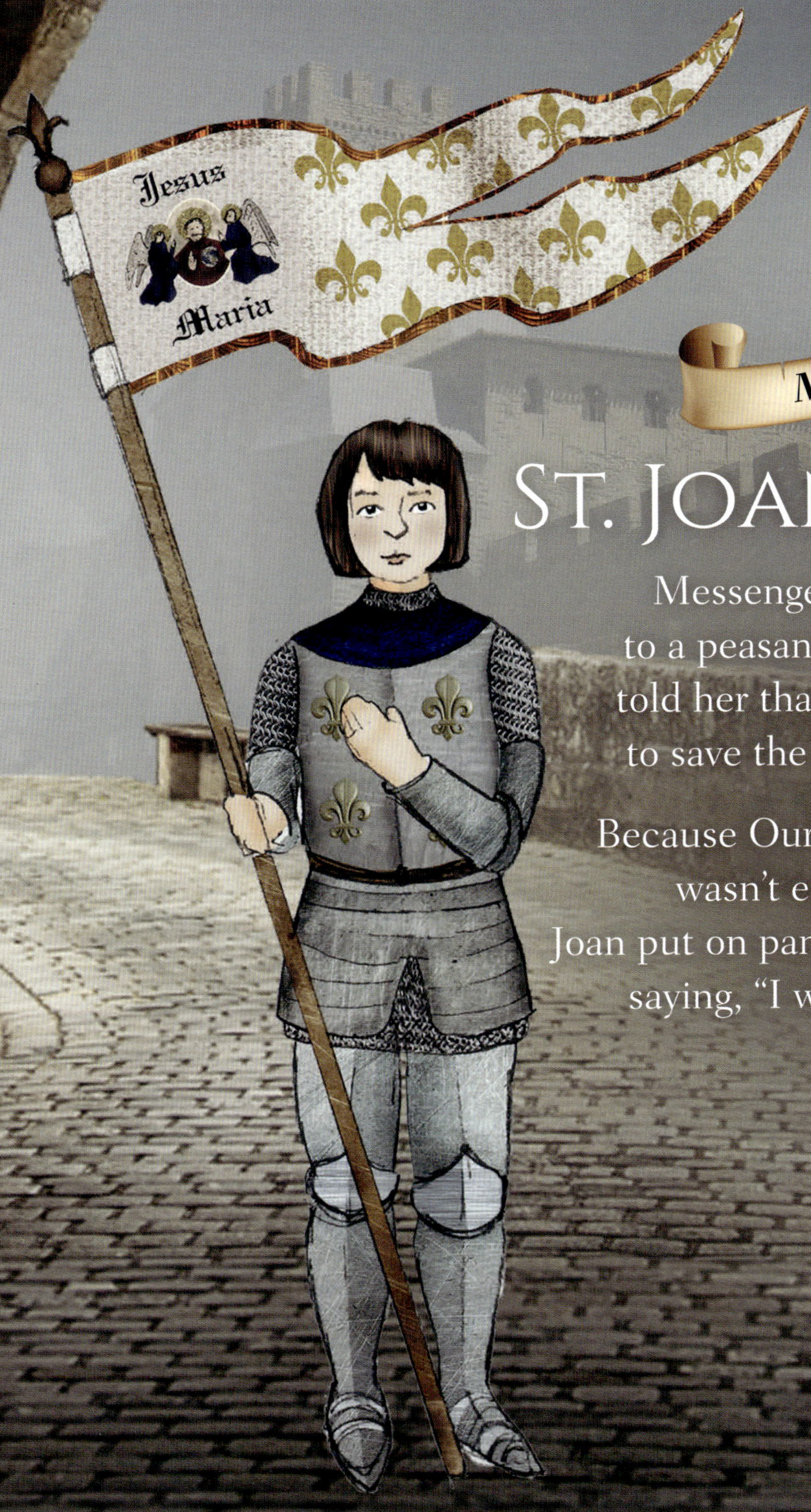

May 30

ST. JOAN OF ARC

Messengers from heaven
to a peasant girl named Joan
told her that God wanted her
to save the country's throne.

Because Our Lord's persistence
wasn't easy to dismiss,
Joan put on pants to fight for France,
saying, "I was born for this!"

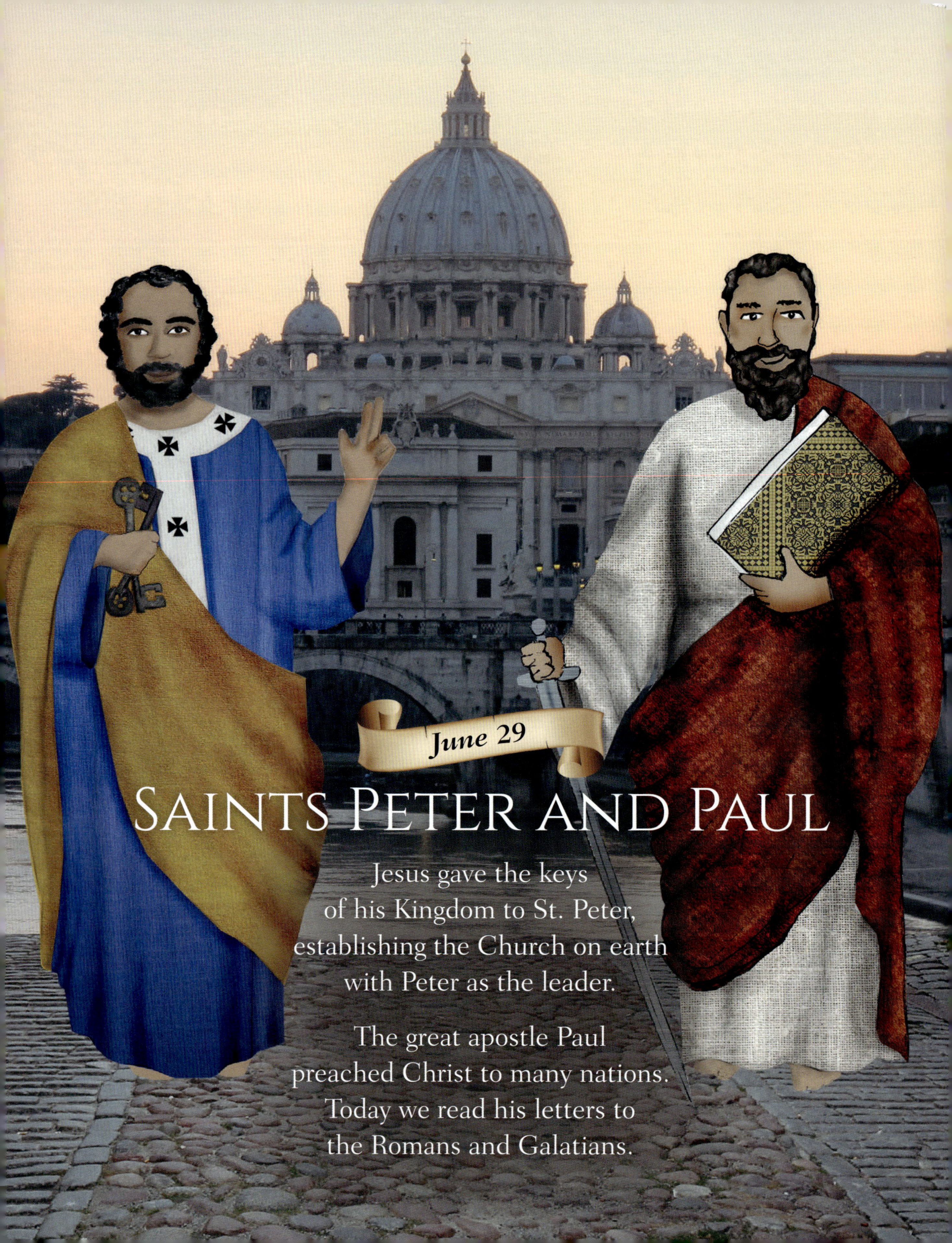

June 29

SAINTS PETER AND PAUL

Jesus gave the keys
of his Kingdom to St. Peter,
establishing the Church on earth
with Peter as the leader.

The great apostle Paul
preached Christ to many nations.
Today we read his letters to
the Romans and Galatians.

St. Kateri Tekakwitha

A native to America,
the daughter of a chief,
Kateri heard the word of God
and came to full belief.

She's patron of creation,
of every rock and tree.
She understood it all reflected
God's divinity.

July 26

Sts. Joachim and Anne

The grandparents of Jesus
were Joachim and Anne.
Their holy marriage made them part
of God's almighty plan.

God blessed them with a child,
so far from ordinary:
the pure and perfect, sinless, spotless
Blessed Virgin Mary.

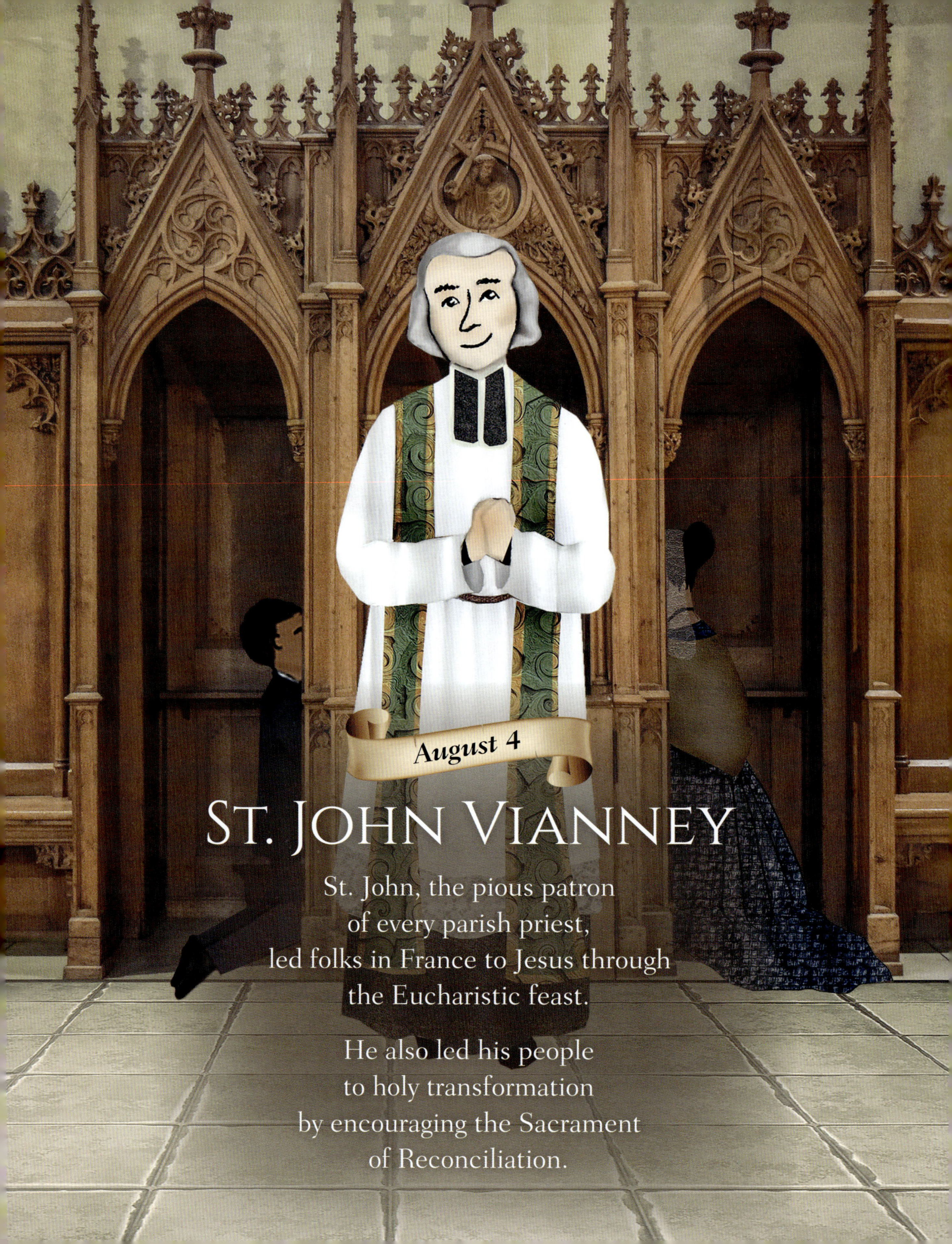

August 4

ST. JOHN VIANNEY

St. John, the pious patron
of every parish priest,
led folks in France to Jesus through
the Eucharistic feast.

He also led his people
to holy transformation
by encouraging the Sacrament
of Reconciliation.

August 23

St. Rose of Lima

To hide her gorgeous features,
Rose rubbed pepper on her face.
In order to help others, she
grew flowers and made lace.

She wore a crown of thorns
and offered up the pain.
She showed that through our crosses, there
are graces to attain.

ave
Maria

September 29

Sts. Michael, Gabriel, and Raphael, Archangels

St. Michael is a fighter
who shields us from temptations.
St. Gabriel brings joyful news
and glad communications.

St. Raphael's the healer,
for he treated Tobit's eyes.
These three are the archangels whom
the Church identifies.

October 4

St. Francis of Assisi

Young Francis was enchanted
with pleasure, wealth, and fame,
till from the chapel crucifix,
Jesus called his name.

He exchanged his fancy clothes
for a simple, humble habit.
He's patron saint of animals —
each turtle, bird, and rabbit.

October 7

OUR LADY OF THE ROSARY

At the Battle of Lepanto,
Our Lady sent her aid
when on their knees with rosaries
the faithful Christians prayed.

Can you say "Our Father"
and "Hail Mary," "Glory Be"?
Then it is true that even you
can pray the Rosary!

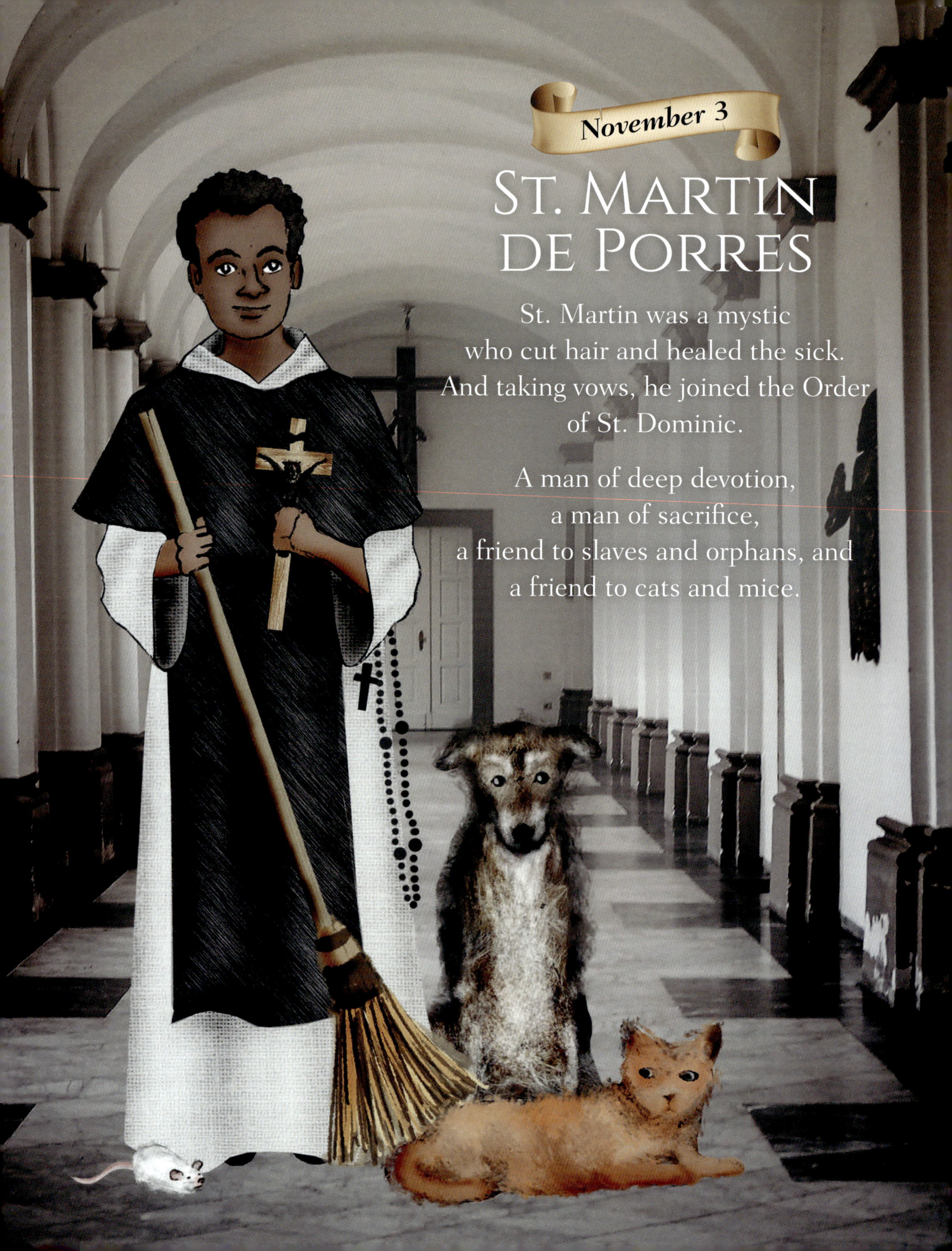

November 3

St. Martin de Porres

St. Martin was a mystic
who cut hair and healed the sick.
And taking vows, he joined the Order
of St. Dominic.

A man of deep devotion,
a man of sacrifice,
a friend to slaves and orphans, and
a friend to cats and mice.

November 22

St. Cecilia

We remember St. Cecilia
as the patron saint of song.
When forced to wed, she bravely said,
"To Jesus I belong."

Within her heart she sang
to God whom she adored.
And through her prayers her husband's heart
converted to the Lord.

December 9

ST. JUAN DIEGO

When Juan went for a walk
in Guadalupe, Mexico,
he startled when he heard a voice —
one he didn't know.

"Build a church right here,
and I'll provide a sign."
And in Juan's cloak Our Lady placed
a miracle design.

December 13

St. Lucy

In Sicily, St. Lucy,
whose name itself means "light,"
is lauded as the patron saint
of blindness, eyes, and sight.

Although a wealthy suitor
wanted Lucy for his wife,
she told the man she had a plan
to give the Lord her life.

St. Agnes

St. Thomas Aquinas

St. Brigid of Ireland

St. Paul Miki and Companions

St. Katharine Drexel

St. Joseph

St. Margaret of Castello

St. George

St. Philip Neri

St. Joan of Arc

Saints Peter and Paul

St. Kateri Tekakwitha

Sts. Joachim and Anne

St. John Vianney

St. Rose of Lima

Archangels

St. Francis of Assisi

Our Lady of the Rosary

St. Martin de Porres

St. Cecilia

St. Juan Diego

St. Lucy

Helping families love and live the Catholic Faith

OSV Kids is an exciting new brand on a mission to help children learn about, live, and love the Catholic Faith. Every OSV Kids product is prayerfully developed to introduce children of all ages to Jesus and his Church. Using beautiful artwork, engaging storytelling, and fun activities, OSV Kids products help families form and develop their Catholic identity and learn to live the faith with great joy.

OSV Kids is a monthly magazine that delivers a fun, trustworthy, and faith-filled set of stories, images, and activities designed to help Catholic families with children ages 2-6 build up their domestic churches and live the liturgical year at home.

OSV Kids books are crafted to inspire and delight kids and parents alike. Each book is designed to kindle the Catholic imagination within young readers through creative storytelling, stunning artwork, and fidelity to the Church's teachings. With board books for infants and toddlers, picture books for young readers, and exciting stories for older kids, OSV Kids has something for everyone in your family.

Learn more at OSVKids.com

About the Author

Meghan Bausch is the author and illustrator of *Saintly Rhymes for Modern Times*. She is also a contributor to *OSV Kids* magazine. During this chaotic season of motherhood, Meghan is elated to have this spiritual and artistic outlet. She lives in Connecticut with her husband and three young children.